Muhammed Oeztuerk
Dorfstr 13
82024 Taufkirchen
Deutschland

CPSIA information can be obtained
at www.ICGtesting.com
Printed in the USA
LVHW051229041119
636244LV00006B/2363

9 781701 34597